1/27/10

Louisburg Library District No. 1
206 S. Broadway St.
Louisburg, KS 66053
913-837-2217
www.louisburglibrary.org

DEMCO

FAVORITE BASKETBALL TEAMS

Dallas Mavericks

Louisburg Library
Bringing People and Information Together

BY ELLEN LABRECQUE

The Child's World®

THE CHILD'S WORLD®
1980 Lookout Drive • Mankato, MN 56003-1705
800-599-READ • www.childsworld.com

ACKNOWLEDGMENTS
The Child's World®: Mary Berendes, Publishing Director
Shoreline Publishing Group, LLC: James Buckley, Jr., Production Director
The Design Lab: Kathleen Petelinsek, Design; Gregory Lindholm, Page Production

PHOTOS
Cover and interior: AP/Wide World Photos

Published in the United States of America.

LIBRARY OF CONGRESS
CATALOGING-IN-PUBLICATION DATA
Labrecque, Ellen.
  Dallas Mavericks / by Ellen Labrecque.
    p. cm. — (Favorite basketball teams)
  Includes bibliographical references and index.
  ISBN 978-1-60253-307-3 (library bound : alk. paper)
  1. Dallas Mavericks (Basketball team)—Juvenile literature.
2. Basketball—Texas—Dallas—Juvenile literature. I. Title. II. Series.
  GV885.52.D34L33 2009
  796.323'6409764'2812—dc22   2009009788

Table of Contents

Go, Mavericks!

The Dallas Mavericks' home is in Texas, the "Lone Star State." The Mavericks also have a team filled with stars! Their fans expect Dallas to play fast and furious basketball, and also have a lot of fun. Are they your favorite team? Let's meet the Dallas Mavericks!

A hand in the face doesn't stop the Mavericks' Jason Terry from making this shot!

6

Josh Howard rises above an **opponent** to make a basket.

Who Are the Mavericks?

The Dallas Mavericks play in the National Basketball Association (NBA). The Mavericks are sometimes called the "Mavs" for short. They are one of 30 teams in the NBA. The NBA includes the Eastern Conference and the Western Conference. The Mavericks play in the Southwest Division of the Western Conference. The Eastern Conference Champion plays the Western Conference Champion in the **NBA Finals**. The Mavericks played in the NBA Finals in 2006. They lost to the Miami Heat, 4–2.

Where They Came From

The Dallas team joined the NBA in 1980. At first, nobody knew what to name them. A local radio station had a "Name the Team" contest. The final choices came down to the Mavericks, Wranglers, and Express. The name Mavericks finally won out! A maverick is someone who does things differently from many other people. The NBA Mavs are the second pro team to play in Dallas. The Chaparrals played in the ABA (American Basketball Association) from 1967 to 1973. They moved to San Antonio. Today, that team is called the Spurs.

9

The Mavericks faced the great "Magic" Johnson in the 1984 playoffs.

10

Dallas takes on San Antonio in a battle from the "Texas Triangle."

Who They Play

The Mavericks play 82 games from October to April. They play every other NBA team at least once. The San Antonio Spurs and the Houston Rockets are the Mavs' two biggest **rivals**. These three teams play in the same division and the same state. Combined, this "Texas Triangle" has played in nine NBA Finals. In 2006, the Mavs faced the Spurs in the Western Conference **Semifinals**. Dallas squeezed by San Antonio, 4 games to 3.

Where They Play

Dallas players live and play in high-flying style! The American Airlines Center is the Mavericks' home. The arena and the locker rooms are the nicest in the NBA. Every player's locker has a flat-screen TV, a DVD player, and a video-game machine! The players also have their own lounge with a pool table and a giant TV. Inside the arena, bench players sit on chairs with comfy cushions. After every game, both teams are offered a giant pile of food.

Mavericks fans love to show off their favorite team colors!

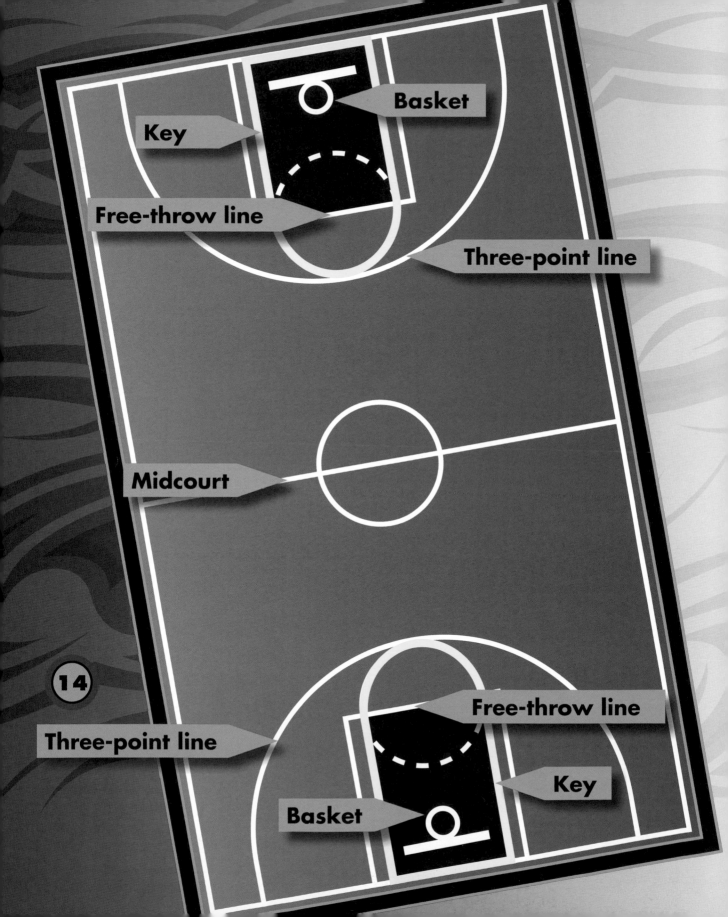

The Basketball Court

Basketball is played on a court made of wood. An NBA court is 94 feet (29 m) long. A painted line shows the middle of the court. Other lines lay out the free-throw area. The space below each basket is known as the "key." The baskets at each end are 10 feet (3 meters) off the ground. The metal rims of the baskets stick out over the court. Nylon nets hang from the rims.

Big Days!

The Dallas Mavericks have never won an NBA title. But they have had plenty of other awesome moments. Here are three of their best:

1984: **The Mavs made the playoffs for the first time. They beat the Seattle SuperSonics in the first round, 3 games to 2. In the final game, they won in overtime, 105–104!**

2001: **Dallas captured the most wins in team history with 57. It was their second season in a row with more than 50 wins.**

2006: **The Mavs made it all the way to the NBA Finals for the first time. They fell to the Miami Heat, 4 games to 2.**

17

Dirk Nowitzki slammed home this basket during the 2006 NBA Finals.

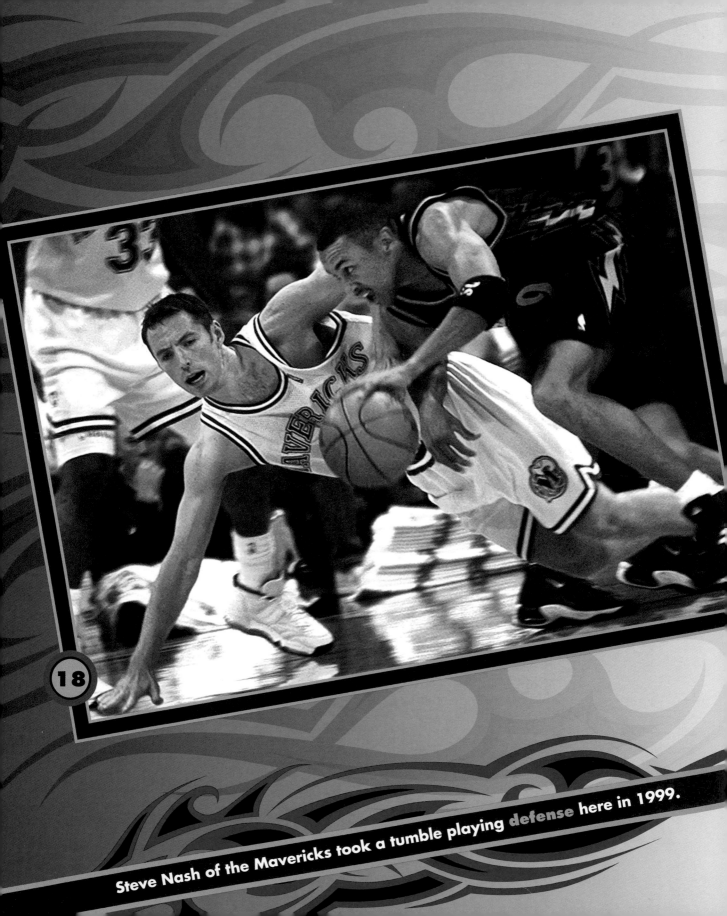

18

Steve Nash of the Mavericks took a tumble playing defense here in 1999.

Tough Days!

Disappointed Dallas fans will tell you that the Mavs have had plenty of luckless seasons. Here are some of their worst:

1981: The Mavericks finished their first season with 15 wins and 67 losses. The good news? They won almost twice as many games the next year.

1992: Dallas finished the season with just 11 wins. It was the second-worst record in NBA history.

1999: The Mavs missed the playoffs for the tenth straight time. But, led by star Dirk Nowitzki, the team was on the rise. The next year, they made it to the second round of the playoffs.

Meet the Fans

Dallas fans love their hoops. But they also support their troops. Fans with front-row seats donate their spots one game a year. They donate them to injured soldiers from the Iraq War. At the game, the soldiers receive loud cheers from the crowds. They get cheers from the Dallas players, too!

21

Mark Cuban not only owns the team . . . he leads the cheers!

Brad Davis used his great dribbling skills to get past defenders.

Heroes Then...

The Mavericks have had some great players.
Brad Davis played on the first Mavericks team
in 1980. He played in Dallas for 12 seasons.
This **guard** was great at making jump shots.
He is one of two Mavs to have his number
retired. That means no other Dallas player
will wear his number, 15. The other player is
Rolando Blackman. "Ro" played alongside
Davis for 11 seasons. He was a star on
offense for Dallas. He often scored lots of
points to help the Mavs win.

Heroes Now...

Dirk Nowitzki is the best-known Mavericks player. He is one of the best seven-foot-tall players ever. The big man shoots a **fade-away jumper** that nobody can defend against. In 2006, Dirk was named the NBA's Most Valuable Player. One of Dirk's teammates is Josh Howard. Howard shuts opponents down with his amazing defense. **Point guard** Jason Kidd gets them both the ball. Kidd passes as if he has eyes all around his head. Jason began his NBA career in Dallas in 1994 and played there until 1997. In 2008, he came back to Dallas again.

Dirk Nowitzki moves very well for such a big player!

25

Gearing Up

Dallas Mavericks players wear a uniform and special basketball sneakers. Some wear other pads to protect themselves. Check out this picture of Dirk Nowitzki and learn about what NBA players wear.

The Basketball

NBA basketballs are made of leather. Several pieces are held together with rubber edges. Inside the leather ball is a hollow ball of rubber. This is filled with air. The leather is covered with little bumps called "pebbles." The pebbles help players get a good grip on the ball. The basketball used in the Women's National Basketball Association (WNBA) is slightly smaller than the men's basketball.

Jersey

Shorts

Knee brace

Socks

Basketball shoes

Dirk Nowitzki wears the Mavericks' dark blue uniform.

Sports Stats

Note: All numbers shown are through the 2008–2009 season.

HIGH SCORERS

These players have scored the most points for the Mavs.

PLAYER	POINTS
Dirk Nowitzki	19,084
Rolando Blackman	16,643

HELPING HAND

Here are Dallas's all-time leaders in **assists**.

PLAYER	ASSISTS
Derek Harper	5,111
Brad Davis	4,524

28

CLEANING THE BOARDS

Rebounds are a big part of the game. Here are the Mavs' best rebounders.

PLAYER	REBOUNDS
Dirk Nowitzki	7,182
James Donaldson	4,589

MOST THREE-POINT SHOTS MADE

Shots taken from behind a line about 23 feet (7 m) from the basket are worth three points. Here are the Mavs' best at these long-distance shots.

PLAYER	THREE-POINT SHOTS
Dirk Nowitzki	1,080
Michael Finley	870

COACH

Who coached the Mavericks to the most wins?

Don Nelson, 339

Glossary

assists passes to teammates that lead directly to making baskets

defense when a team doesn't have the ball and is trying to keep the other team from scoring

fade-away jumper a shot that a player takes while jumping backward

guard one of two players who set up plays, pass to teammates closer to the basket, and shoot from farther away

NBA Finals the seven-game NBA championship series, in which the champion must win four games

offense when a team has the ball and is trying to score

opponent someone a team or person is competing against

playoffs a series of games between 16 teams that decide which two teams will play in the NBA Finals

point guard the team's main ball handler, who brings the ball up the court and sets up the offense

rebounds missed shots that bounce off the backboard or rim and are often grabbed by another player

rivals teams that play each other often and have an ongoing competition

semifinals the final round of the playoffs, with the winners going on to play in the final game or series

Find Out More

Books

Christopher, Matt. *Greatest Moments in Basketball History*. New York: Little, Brown, 2009.

Craats, Rennay. *Basketball*. Toronto: Weigl Publishers, 2008.

Hareas, John. *Eyewitness Basketball*. New York: DK, 2005.

McRae, Sloane. *Dirk Nowitzki*. New York: PowerKids Press, 2009.

Web Sites

Visit our Web page for links about the Dallas Mavericks and other NBA teams:

childsworld.com/links

Note to Parents, Teachers, and Librarians: We routinely verify our Web links to make sure they are safe, active sites—so encourage your readers to check them out!

Index

ELLEN LABRECQUE

Ellen Labrecque has written books for young readers on basketball, tennis, ice hockey, and other sports. Ellen used to work for *Sports Illustrated Kids* magazine and has written about many NBA stars. She likes to watch basketball. The Philadelphia 76ers are her favorite team.